31 Days
of
Poetry Prompts

9
more words

Jim Russo

& Nita

ACKNOWLEDGMENTS

A big shout out to:

Poetry Santa Cruz
Willow Glen Poetry Project of San Jose
Sparring with Beatnik Ghosts of Santa Cruz

Author photo on back cover by Todd Russo

Author inquiries and mail orders:

Available on amazon.com

Sky Bolt Circus Press
2510 Soquel Ave, Suite 211
Santa Cruz, CA 95062

facebook.com/CentralCoastPoetryShows
www. CentralCoastPoetryShows.com

OTHER BOOKS BY THIS AUTHOR

Soldiers for Peace & Kids Ruled

Sway of Color & Laura

I Wanna Hold Your Hand & Make Your Move

***

31 Days of Poetry Prompts: Grief & Loss

31 Days of Poetry Prompts: Humanity

31 Days of Poetry Prompts: Reflections

31 Days of Poetry Prompts: for Young Poets

31 Days of Poetry Prompts: Love & Romance

31 Days of Poetry Prompts: 5 Words

31 Days of Poetry Prompts: 7 Words

31 Days of Poetry Prompts: 9 Words

31 Days of Poetry Prompts: 11 Words

31 Days of Poetry Prompts: 5 More Words

31 Days of Poetry Prompts: 7 More Words

As we must account for every idle word, so must we account for every idle silence.

-Benjamin Franklin

TIPS & CHALLENGES

31 Days of Poetry Prompts is part journal, part workbook, and a whole lot of fun. Sit down and relax, we did the hard part, we removed the blank page that seems to block creativity, so now all you have to do is be inspired by the daily prompts.
Challenge your creative skills with these fun, evocative, and interesting words that will guarantee your poetry will reflect those qualities as well

Poetry Prompt tips:
1. Many prompt words are both verbs and nouns. Explore the bonus possibilities of these double-duty words, like read, lead, nurse, lumber, mint, etc.
2. All forms of a word can be used: trying pluralizing your nouns, creating adverbs, and past, present and future tenses.

Poetry Prompt Challenges:
1. Create the shortest poem possible using all the prompt words
2. Start or end each line with a prompt word
3. Alphabetize the prompt words and then use them in order (or reverse order)

We've provided extra pages at the end so you can experiment with your own prompts.
We hope you enjoy this series.

Day 2 Prompt: **hurricane autumn scarlet valley hidden linen banjo above fly**

Day 3 Prompt: **cartwheel southern avocado tequila parrot night house haunt rust**

Day 5 Prompt: **sanctuary midnight coyote window within climb mercy nest dead**

 Wednesday chicken flower shiver beside charm birth clue loft

 sunrise beneath prairie calico starve blame mist buzz cat

 November starlight raccoon chimney capture country across reason four

 boulevard bedtime gentle cherish spoon sleet wild blue by

 treasure summer sundial below harbor starry blaze noble snake

Day 19 Prompt: **crossroad evening village storm laugh shun high wren joy**

Day 19 Prompt: **crossroad evening village storm laugh shun high wren joy**

 lantern viaduct willow never proud ahead gnaw slam lynx

 persnickety Saturday umbrella cheetah silence flower before forest cry

 lagoon awaken sunset yearn dirty weeds lamp jay up

Day 27 Prompt: **bamboo sorrow forgive corner around thirst music later panda**

 terrace wither worm patch down glow May elm nap

 minute inside stamp porch mourn grace silk dew bee

Day 31 Prompt: **northern sparrow discover bramble abrasive river bells pain year**

Now write some more!

ABOUT THE AUTHOR

Jim is a narrative poet, a storyteller with a sense of humor. Jim believes it's every artist's calling to observe and comment.

He is host of the local TV show— Central Coast Poetry Shows.